The Real Blues

By Betsy Hannah

Edited by Robert Pace

12-BAR BLUES IN 12 EASY STEPS

PRIMARY TRIADS

First, look at the triads (3 note chords) shown below as they appear on each degree of the C *major* scale. Notice that the I, IV and V chords (called "primary triads") are each "major."

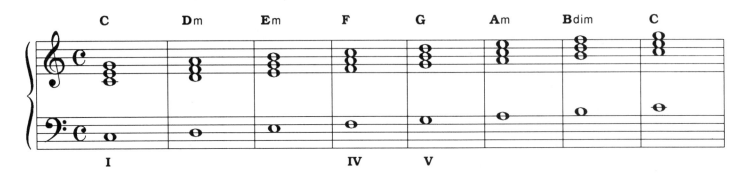

These three chords (the I, IV, and V) are all you need to begin improvising the Blues, which is a 12-bar pattern with 4 beats per bar.

Memorize these patterns:

A. Numbers Only	B. Numbers with Letters	C. Letters Only

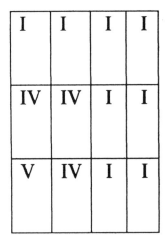

I	I	I	I
IV	IV	I	I
V	IV	I	I

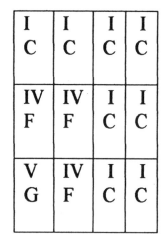

I	I	I	I
C	C	C	C
IV	IV	I	I
F	F	C	C
V	IV	I	I
G	F	C	C

C	C	C	C
F	F	C	C
G	F	C	C

Eventually try these in all keys. If you practice thinking the numbers first, it will be easier to transpose to other keys. Transpose first to the standard keys of F and Bb (to play with wind instruments). Then add D, A and G (to play with guitars). Listen to CD Track 2 as you study this page.

BASIC BLUES FORM

Although there are different patterns or *progressions* which are frequently used in the Blues, the most basic one uses only the I, IV, and V chords. After you develop the ability to identify this chord progression easily, you can learn new chords and other progressions.

Here is the chord sequence for Basic Blues Improvisation which you should memorize:

I	I	I	I	IV	IV	I	I	V	IV	I	I (V)
C	C	C	C	F	F	C	C	G	F	C	C (G)

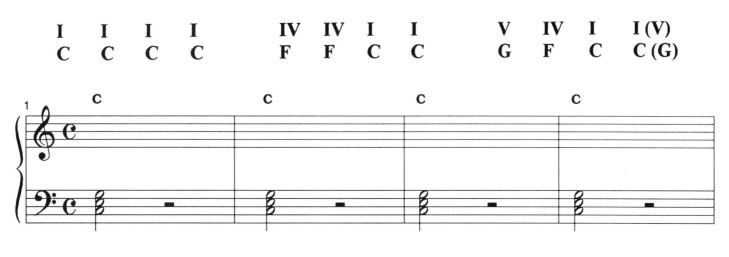

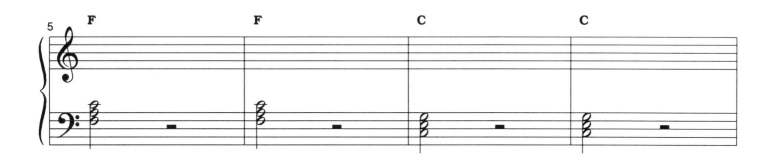

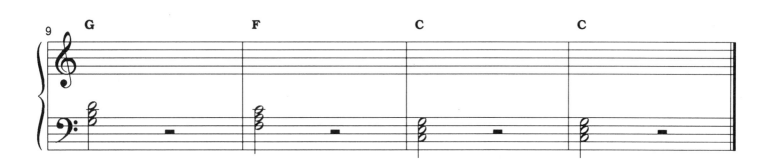

To use your CD as a "practice partner," play Track 3. The first chorus will give you the chords, then a second chorus allows you to supply to the chords a shown above. You will hear four "taps" as an introduction.

DOMINANT 7THS

Most *Blues* chords are "Dominant" 7ths. To make a dominant out of any major triad, just add the note that is a minor 7th above the root or one whole step below the octave.

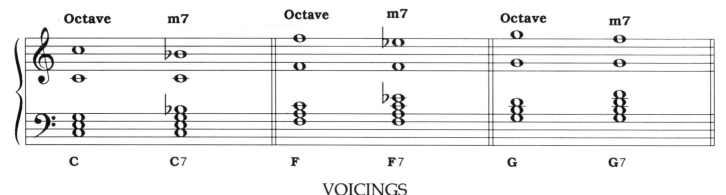

VOICINGS

Basic "Hip" voicings of these chords use only 2 tones of each chord (the 3rd and 7th).

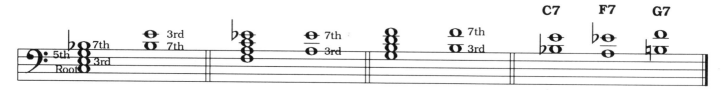

"COMP"

The following left hand chords provide a perfect "comp" sound for both the beginning and advanced performer. Before playing the CD, find your finger position on the keyboard. Then, listen to the CD, Track 4 and be ready to play either hand on the second chorus. You will hear a 2-bar introduction.

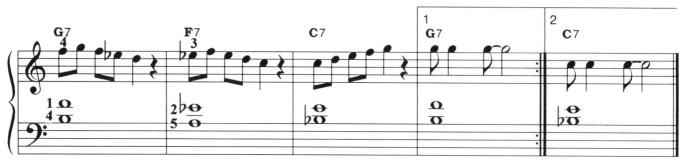

BLUES MOTIVES

Use this form to create your *Blues* compositions. Each Roman numeral represents a 4-beat measure or *bar*. Your melodic pattern in the right hand should last 5 to 7 beats. Create other motives and play them through this structure. It will lead you to an "in-hand" series of phrases, or *licks*, that you will be able to use in free improvisation.

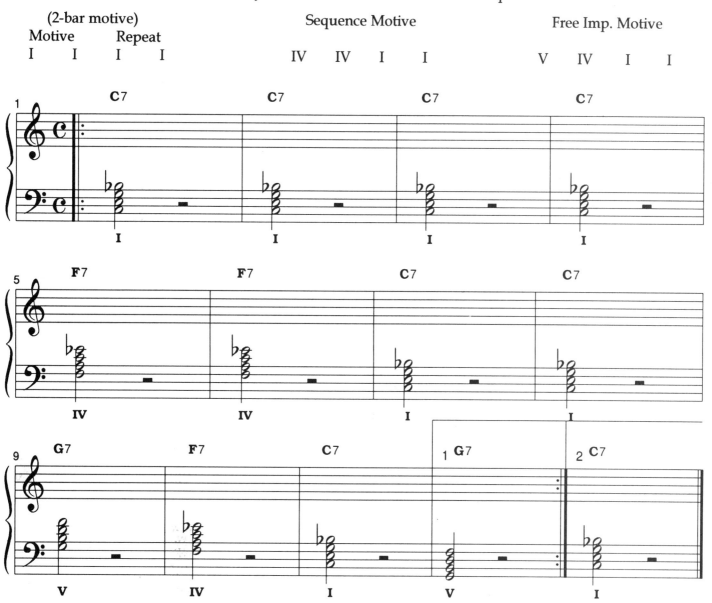

Create melodic motives using these scales:

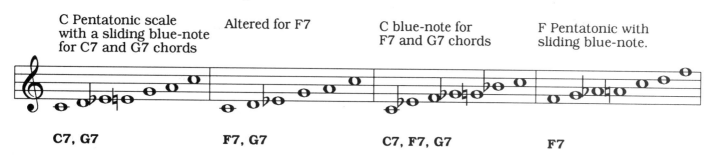

C Pentatonic scale with a sliding blue-note for C7 and G7 chords	Altered for F7	C blue-note for F7 and G7 chords	F Pentatonic with sliding blue-note.
C7, G7	**F7, G7**	**C7, F7, G7**	**F7**

CD Practice, Track 5: (8 beat music intro) The first chorus demonstrates a motive following the form described above. On the second chorus, play a motive you have created. You may also use motives from pages 6-9.

5-FINGER SCALE PATTERNS

This example follows the 12-bar blues form.

Quickly find the following:

- a) 5 note pattern going up, followed by an inversion in the next bar.
- b) Repetition of the 2-bar pattern in bar 3-4 and 7-8.
- c) Transposition of this pattern in bar 5-6.
- d) New pattern and sequence in bar 9 and 10.
- e) Cadence in bar 11-12.

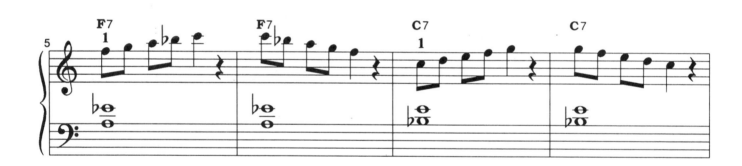

CD Practice, Track 6: (4 tap intro) Just listen to the "lazy triplet" sound (the 8th notes are not quite even) of the scale patterns in the first chorus. Then, play RH the second time. Repeat this track playing first one hand alone, then the other until you can play them easily.

CHORD TONE MOTIVE USING "SEQUENCE"

The chord tone melody has added the lower 3rd to create a "bluesy" sound.
Before playing it, look for these melodic, rhythmic, and harmonic patterns:

a)   Bars 1 and 2 are repeated in bars 3 and 4.
b)   Melodic pattern moves up in bar 5 because of harmonic change and is
     repeated beginning on F.
c)   Melodic pattern returns to original position (bar 7)
d)   One-bar sequence matches chord changes in bars 9 and 10.

CD Practice, Track 7: (4 tap intro) Listen to the first chorus several times, then put the RH
   chord-tone motive with it. Repeat the RH motive on the second chorus. Replay the entire
   track several times to gain skill in playing both hands together with the background.

STAYING IN PLACE

In this example of the 12-bar blues, the right hand follows a 5-note pattern for the first 8 bars. In bars 5 and 6, the 3rd (middle note) is lowered to E♭ to match the F7 chord. Bars 9 and 10 outline a different 4-note pattern followed by the return of the original 5-note pattern in bar 11. The eighth notes may be syncopated by playing them as triplets, "lazy triplets."

CD Practice, Track 8: (4 tap intro) The first chorus is played as written. The second chorus is background only. Repeat both tracks until you can play hands together easily. Then create your own motive which "stays in place," then use that motive on the second chorus.

PLAYING A "RIFF"

A "Riff" is the exact same motive repeated throughout the blues pattern. Here the motive is used as a "Riff" and changes notes only to match chord changes. Syncopate the melodic pattern with the "lazy triplet."

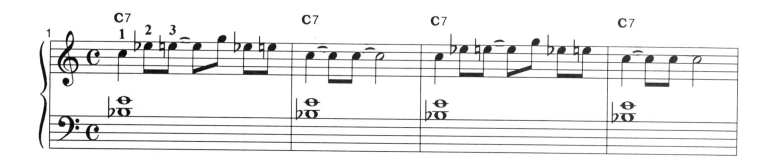

CD Practice, Track 9: (4 tap intro) Practice playing your RH "Riff" alone with the first chorus, and as a solo on the second chorus. Eventually play both hands and create new "Riffs" for the second chorus.

SCALES FOR BLUE MOTIVES

The following examples show how a simple 5-tone Pentatonic pattern may be altered with a blue note and combined with the modes. There are also examples of the "Blue-Note" scale. Play each of these several times to become familiar with its sound. CD Track 10 introduces these scales.

1. Pentatonic   2. Pentatonic with added Blue-note (Eb)   3. Pentatonic/Mixolydian Combination (Bb added)

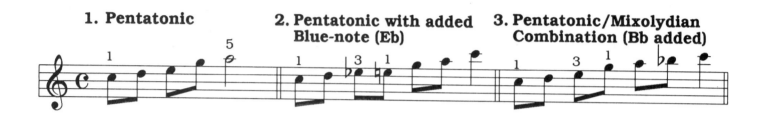

4. Combination Pentatonic/ Blue-note/Mixolydian   5. Mixolydian

6. Blue-note

7. Blue-note: whole octave

CHORD TONE MOTIVE
(Expanded)

Here is an example of the pentatonic motive with slight expansions.

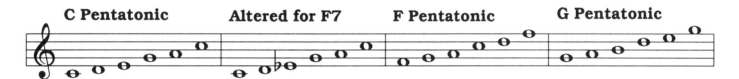

In this "Riff" the motive is repeated "in place," changing notes only in bar 5 to match the Eb of the F7 chord.

CD Practice, Track 11: (4 tap intro) Listen and practice until you can play along with the first chorus. On the second chorus, play both hands with background and repeat this until it is easy. After that, play your own improvisation with the second chorus.

THE BLUE NOTE SCALE

First play the 12-bar blues example below, then use either the "5-finger blues scale" or the "full octave blue note scale" to create your own melodic variations for this riff.

5-finger Blue-note scale   **Full octave Blue-note scale**

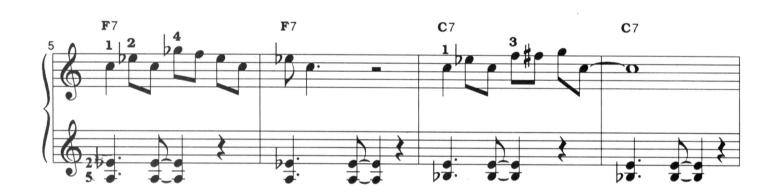

CD Practice, Track 12: (4 tap intro) Practice playing just the RH motive with the first chorus, then do hands together on the second chorus. Eventually create new blue-note motives to play with the second chorus.

"CHARLESTON COMP"

This basic "Charleston" rhythm will sound good anywhere! Use the syncopated rhythm in it to improvise many "jazzy" syncopated chord patterns. Once you can play this, it will become easy to construct a "walking bass" line.

CD Practice, Track 13: (4 tap intro) First, play along with the "Charleston Comp" on both choruses. Notice the added base pattern on the second chorus. You can use this entire track as background to practice new RH motives.

"CHARLESTON COMP" VARIATION

The F7 chord as it appears in the second bar is another frequently used blues progression.

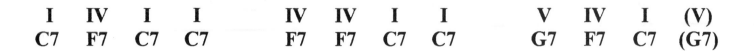

I	IV	I	I		IV	IV	I	I		V	IV	I	(V)
C7	F7	C7	C7		F7	F7	C7	C7		G7	F7	C7	(G7)

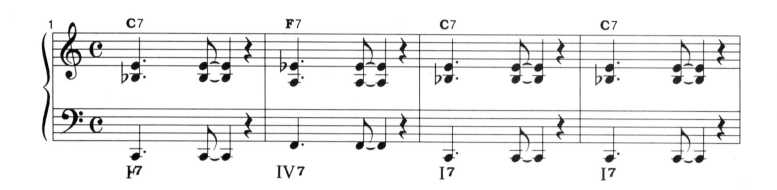

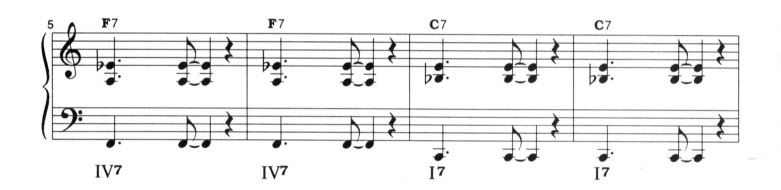

CD Practice, Track 14: (4 tap intro) First listen to the "Charleston" Comp which accompanies the melody in the first chorus. Then on the second chorus you provide the comp.

ADDING THE IV CHORD

(Chord variation)

Here is another commonly used blues progression (as introduced on p. 14). Notice that the F7 chord (IV 7) appears initially in the second bar, then again in the 5th, 6th and 9th bars.

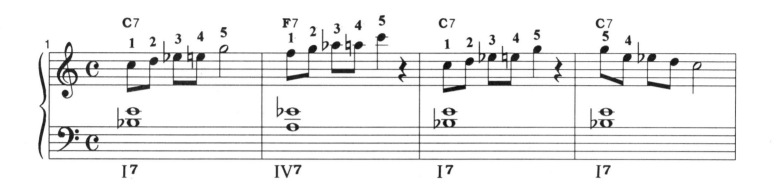

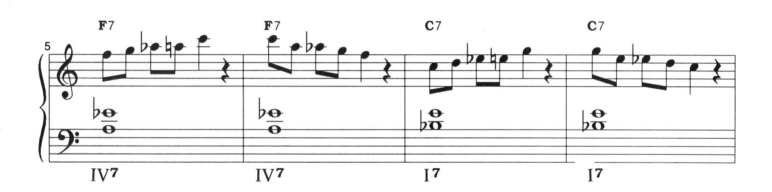

CD Practice, Track 15: (4 tap intro) Listen to the first chorus several times then play along with it. Play the RH melodic part alone on the second chorus. Eventually play your own motive/improvisation on the second chorus.

THE "INSTANT COMP"

Use a walking bass line in the LH with these inversions of the 7th chords in the RH.

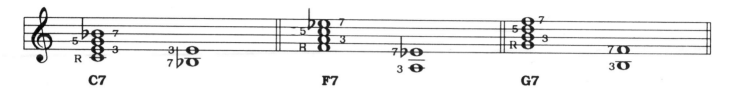

CD Practice, Track 16: (4 tap intro) The first chorus is the instant comp as written. You may play LH, RH, or both during either chorus.

COMBO TIME

1. First play the LH pattern with the instant comp.
2. Leave out the comp and play the bass pattern with the RH melody.
3. If you can get a partner, play all three parts together.

CD Practice, Track 17: (4 tap intro) On the first chorus you can play either part to get practice in keeping the music "going." The second chorus provides opportunities to create new Blue-note melodic patterns.

2386

"SWING" CHORD COMP

By adding the 6th to the C chord and the 9th to the F and G chord, the comp has a "swing" sound.

CD Practice, Track 18: (4 tap intro) Use track one for practice in learning to play the LH bass pattern. When this seems easy, add the RH chords.

COMBO TIME

First, play the one bar bass pattern with the RH comp as written, then repeat with melodic variations in alternate measures.

CD Practice, Track 19: (8 tap intro) In the first chorus, play the LH alone, then when this seems easy, add the RH comp. Also, in the beginning you can play RH variations alone over the bass part. Eventually, RH melody and the LH bass pattern create a "solo" style.

ROCKIN' BASS

Try this new bass pattern in combo with the RH comp, minus the melodic pattern. Next, leave out the comp and play the melodic pattern and bass. If you wish, you may leave out the bass part to concentrate on the new melody. Notice the change to the IV chord in the 5th bar.

CD Practice, Track 20: (8 tap intro) On first chorus, concentrate on the new "rock" bass pattern and add the comp when this seems easy. You may also practice the RH melody. On the second chorus, play the LH rock bass with the RH comp chords.

CREATE YOUR OWN

Try the RH comp chords over the new LH bass pattern. Again, you may omit the RH chords and substitute the blues melody above that. Improvise new blue note melodies by changing the direction of the melody or repeating some of the tones. Remember to keep it simple!

CD Practice, Track 21: (8 tap intro) First chorus is the full combo as written, second chorus demonstrates melodic improvisation and variations on the comp chords. Practice the different parts until you can play along.

SWINGING COMBO

Here is a two-hand swing comp using a 5-tone scale. Notice the similarities in the first four bars, then the next four bars. Bars 1 and 2 are repeated sequentially in bars 5 and 6. Bars 7 and 8 are exact repetitions of bars 3 and 4. Bars 9 and 10 move in a downward sequence into bars 11 and 12.

CD Practice, Track 22: (16 tap (4 bar) intro) The first chorus is as written. Practice any combination of the three parts. The second chorus demonstrates RH improvisation, and you can practice the two-hand accompaniment.

Here the melody has thirds (double notes) for the top part above the chords of the comp and the bass pattern. Because of the double notes in the RH, this will sound good even without the middle chords if you want to try it as a solo.

CD Practice, Track 23: (8 tap intro) The first chorus demonstrates piano solo with just rhythm back-up. The second chorus demonstrates RH variations on the 3rds and a second instrument coming in with secondary improvisation. Use this track to learn this style.